NATIONAL
SINGLE WINDOW

GUIDANCE NOTE

MAY 2022

IAN DEVELOPMENT BANK

Creative Commons Attribution 3.0 IGO license (CC BY 3.0 IGO)

© 2022 Asian Development Bank
6 ADB Avenue, Mandaluyong City, 1550 Metro Manila, Philippines
Tel +63 2 8632 4444; Fax +63 2 8636 2444
www.adb.org

Some rights reserved. Published in 2022.

ISBN 978-92-9269-495-1 (print); 978-92-9269-496-8 (electronic); 978-92-9269-497-5 (ebook)
Publication Stock No. TIM220175-2
DOI: http://dx.doi.org/10.22617/TIM220175-2

Corrigenda to ADB publications may be found at http://www.adb.org/publications/corrigenda.

Notes:
In this publication, "$" refers to United States dollars, unless otherwise stated.
ADB recognizes "China" as the People's Republic of China; "Hong Kong" as Hong Kong, China; and "Korea" as the Republic of Korea.

Cover design by Leslie Lim.

Contents

Table, Figures, and Boxes

Abbreviations

ADB	Asian Development Bank
ASEAN	Association of Southeast Asian Nations
ASW	ASEAN Single Window
B2B	business–to–business
B2G	business–to–government
BPR	business process redesign
CBRA	cross-border regulatory agency
CMS	customs management system
EIF	European Interoperability Framework
EU	European Union
ICT	information and communication technology
KPI	key performance indicator
LPCO	license, permit, certificate, other
NSW	national single window
PCS	port community system
PMU	project management unit
SLA	service-level agreement
SWII	single window international interoperability
TFA	trade facilitation agreement
UN/CEFACT	United Nations Centre for Trade Facilitation and Electronic Business
UNCTAD	United Nations Conference on Trade and Development
UNESCAP	United Nations Economic and Social Commission for Asia and the Pacific
UNNExT	United Nations Network of Experts for Paperless Trade and Transport in Asia and the Pacific
WCO	World Customs Organization
WTO	World Trade Organization

Executive Summary

The national single window (NSW) enables an environment for traders and transport service providers to interact efficiently with cross-border regulatory agencies (CBRAs) in international trade. Traders and their agents benefit from the convenience of transacting with CBRAs electronically via the NSW. Procedures are simplified and streamlined since CBRAs operate in a coordinated manner, automated data exchange eliminates the need for submission of duplicate information, and automated processing speeds up end-to-end processing of import and export transactions. CBRAs benefit from tighter border control, improved efficiency, and greater ability to monitor performance against service-level agreements. The NSW's objective is to reduce the time and cost of international trade transactions.

While the NSW concept is simple, its implementation is complex since it involves many CBRAs, transport operators, cargo handlers, commercial banks, and the central bank. Governance is most effective when led by a steering committee of senior decision makers. Several working groups are required to tackle design and implementation. An effective NSW environment needs to manage several design components: business process redesign, data harmonization, and improvements to the legal framework to support changes and new modes of operation. Business process redesign is critical to streamline procedures and leverage the capabilities of the NSW to automate data exchange and expedite automated processing. Changing procedures and computer systems by so many stakeholders is a challenge and needs strong political commitment, which can be best achieved by an influential project champion who will mobilize stakeholders to coordinate. Experienced project management is essential to plan, coordinate, and oversee the execution of multiple parallel projects. A comprehensive capacity-building program is required to prepare the NSW project team for design and implementation activities. Private sector stakeholders are the main users of the NSW and possess practical on-the-ground knowledge of procedural issues and workable solutions. Collaboration and involvement of the private sector throughout design and implementation are essential to create an effective NSW environment.

The NSW is executed in phases given the complexity of the features and interfaces to be implemented across many stakeholders. Each country has its specific operating environment and priorities for trade facilitation, and each NSW implementation is unique. Government will need to appoint an entity responsible for operating the NSW. The decision is driven by the country-specific context, and NSW operators worldwide are almost evenly split between government entities and private sector institutions. Government will have to decide on the business model to ensure the sustainability of the NSW: government funding or payment by users for NSW services. NSWs worldwide have adopted both.

Interest is increasing in single window international interoperability to boost regional trade. The Association of Southeast Asian Nations (ASEAN) Single Window was initiated in 2005 and started operating in 2018. The experience of the Pacific Alliance (Chile, Republic of Colombia, Mexico, and Peru) was simpler, with single window international interoperability implemented by 2016, within 2 years after the decision to proceed, thanks to Inter-American Development Bank financial assistance and technical support.

Introduction

The United Nations Centre for Trade Facilitation and Electronic Business (UN/CEFACT) Recommendation No. 33 defines a "single window" as a "facility that allows parties involved in trade and transport to lodge standardized information and documents with a single entry point to fulfil all import, export, and transit-related regulatory requirements. If information is electronic, then individual data elements should only be submitted once."[1]

A single window provides a unified electronic interface to interact with customs and other regulatory agencies involved in cross-border trade and transit. The single window obviates the need for traders to separately file declarations and seek clearance from multiple agencies. Clearances from multiple regulatory agencies are obtained on the same electronic platform. Government agencies can maintain control and monitor compliance more effectively. Processing international trade through a single window reduces cargo release time and the cost of doing business, increases competitiveness and trade efficiency, and improves the way business is done.

However, implementing the single window has challenges, chief of which is consensus building among agencies, interagency differences in degree of automation, and data requirements and sustainability.

Given the number of agencies involved, establishing a single window calls for finding a "champion" at higher levels of government, identifying a lead agency, setting up coordinating structures, and designing a business model. Adopting global standards in data and messaging ease designing information and communication technology (ICT).

The World Trade Organization (WTO) Trade Facilitation Agreement (TFA), Article 10.4 requires member countries to "endeavor to establish or maintain a single window, enabling traders to submit documentation and/or data requirements for importation, exportation, or transit of goods through a single entry point to the participating authorities or agencies."[2] The World Customs Organization (WCO) has used its resources to plan and implement single windows. While global resources are immensely helpful, the facility should be customized to each country's capacity and economic needs.

This guidance note helps Asian Development Bank (ADB) developing member countries and staff plan, prepare, and implement electronic national single window (NSW) systems for international trade.

The guidance note has five parts: explanation of the NSW, why the NSW matters, what its key governance and design components are, implications of single window international interoperability (SWII), and good practice and risk mitigation.

---

[1] UN/CEFACT. 2005. *Recommendation No. 33: Recommendation and Guidelines on Establishing a Single Window.* Geneva. p. 3. https://unece.org/DAM/cefact/recommendations/rec33/rec33_trd352e.pdf.
[2] WTO. 2014. *Trade Facilitation Agreement.* Article 10.4.1. p. 15. https://docs.wto.org/dol2fe/Pages/SS/directdoc.aspx?filename=q:/WT/L/940.pdf&Open=True.

Understanding the National Single Window

The National Single Window (NSW) is one system interconnected with international trade and transport stakeholders to fulfill all import, export, and transit border control procedures. Government border control agencies are linked to the NSW to process transactions but operate in the background. International trade and transport stakeholders transact with border control agencies via only one system, thus the term "single window."

The NSW is a highly convenient tool for private sector stakeholders since all information associated with a trade or related transport transactions is submitted and retrieved from a single system. Private sector stakeholders reap the benefits of electronic access: savings in time and resources since physical submission and collection of documents are eliminated.

The NSW is a powerful tool for government authorities. It is highly versatile and flexible and can implement a wide variety of trade facilitation measures. The World Trade Organization (WTO) Trade Facilitation Agreement (TFA) articles on transparency, efficiency, and predictability can be implemented via the NSW. Its power arises from its capabilities for information sharing, event tracking, automated processing, and information exchange with other stakeholders and stakeholder systems once it receives an incoming transaction.

NSW implementation is unique for each country since the NSW must invariably adapt to the prevailing ecosystem for trade and transport, priorities for reform, and resource constraints. There is no one-size-fits-all solution. In preparing for the NSW, a variable geometry design must be adopted as well as a gradual, phased rollout to manage the inherent complexity of implementing the NSW. WCO surveys in 2011 and 2016 show that single window projects were implemented in phases that were sometimes longer than 5 years.[3] No country has ever implemented a full-fledged NSW at once.

Paperless trade to simplify and streamline processing of border control procedures for international trade started with the Nippon Airport Cargo Community System in Japan in 1978.[4] Using the same concept of one central computer system linked to all public and private sector stakeholders for international trade procedures, Singapore implemented the well-known TradeNet system in 1989.[5] In 2005, the United Nations Centre for Trade Facilitation and Electronic Business (UN/CEFACT) first used the term "single window" in its often quoted Recommendation No. 33 (footnote 1).

Parties involved in NSW trade and transport include importers; exporters; ship agents; airlines; sea container terminal handlers; airport terminals; rail depots; and special zones under customs control, including bonded warehouses, special economic zones, export processing zones, and free ports.

---

[3] WCO. 2011. A Survey of Single Window Implementation. *WCO Research Paper*. 17.
[4] United Nations Network of Experts for Paperless Trade and Transport in Asia and the Pacific. 2011. *Japan's Development of a Single Window—Case of Nippon Airport Cargo Community System*. Bangkok.
[5] Harvard Business School. 1995. *Singapore TradeNet: A Tale of One City*. Cambridge, MA.

Figure 1 illustrates the NSW environment and common stakeholders. Private sector stakeholders either sign on to the NSW to submit transactions or transmit electronic messages to it. Similarly, cross-border regulatory agencies (CBRAs) interact with the NSW either via their in-house system, such as a customs management system, or, if a CBRA has no computerized system, CBRA staff log in directly to the NSW to process border control documents received from traders or their representatives. The NSW environment is thus flexible in accommodating CBRAs with different levels of computerization and it is not mandatory for a CBRA to computerize its border control services to participate in the NSW environment. The government decides which entity is responsible for operating the NSW and the chosen operator can be either a private or government entity.

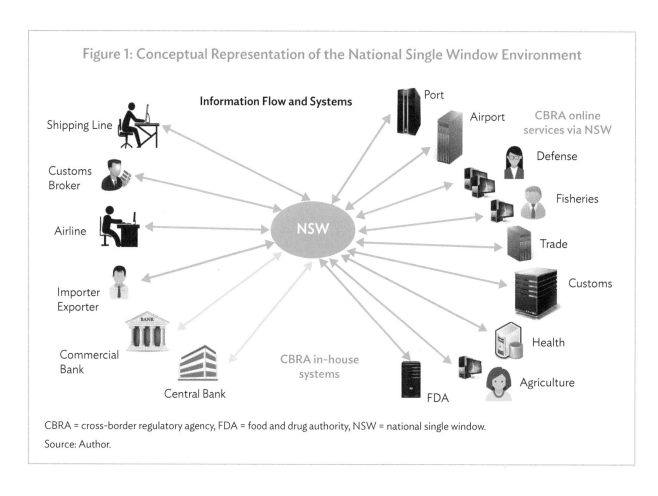

Figure 1: Conceptual Representation of the National Single Window Environment

CBRA = cross-border regulatory agency, FDA = food and drug authority, NSW = national single window.
Source: Author.

It is important to highlight that the UN/CEFACT definition of the NSW covers interactions between traders, logistics service providers, cargo handlers, and government regulatory agencies. The NSW is thus an instance of business-to-government (B2G) e-government as well as government-to-government (G2G) e-government. Traders and cargo handlers transact with government (B2G) and government agencies transact with other government agencies (G2G). Business-to-business (B2B) transactions are, therefore, not covered in this definition. Electronic payment, as a specialized banking transaction from trader to government bank, is highly desirable to speed up payment of fees to government agencies that intervene throughout the cycle of trade procedures.

WTO has embraced the single window concept. TFA Article 10.4 provides clear direction (footnote 2). The TFA database in July 2021 listed 81 countries with NSWs at different stages of implementation.[6]

The term single window is, in some ways, a misnomer since the term "facility" in UN/CEFACT Recommendation No. 33 is often associated with "system." The single window system on its own is of limited use. The fundamental benefit arises from the single window interacting electronically with other stakeholder systems, creating an environment with the potential to implement multiple trade facilitation measures. World Customs Organization (WCO), as in Figure 2, thus proposes useful terminology distinctions with the single window concept, progressing to single window initiative and eventual implementation of a single window environment.[7]

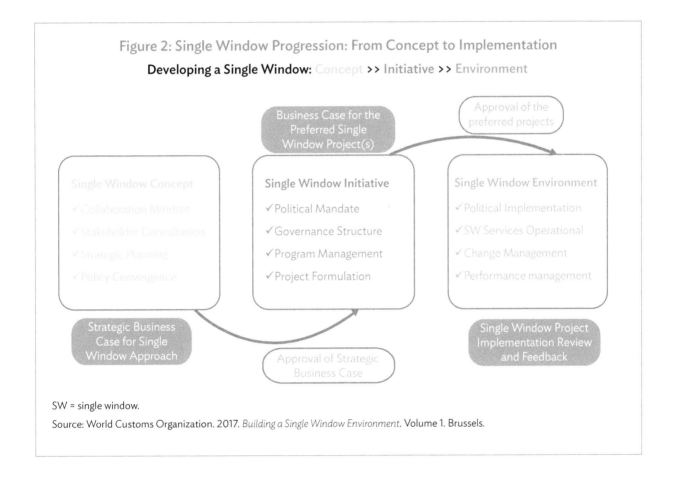

Figure 2: Single Window Progression: From Concept to Implementation

Developing a Single Window: Concept >> Initiative >> Environment

Business Case for the Preferred Single Window Project(s)

Approval of the preferred projects

Single Window Concept
✓ Collaboration Mindset
✓ Stakeholder Consultation
✓ Strategic Planning
✓ Policy Convergence

Single Window Initiative
✓ Political Mandate
✓ Governance Structure
✓ Program Management
✓ Project Formulation

Single Window Environment
✓ Political Implementation
✓ SW Services Operational
✓ Change Management
✓ Performance management

Strategic Business Case for Single Window Approach

Approval of Strategic Business Case

Single Window Project Implementation Review and Feedback

SW = single window.

Source: World Customs Organization. 2017. *Building a Single Window Environment*. Volume 1. Brussels.

WCO describes the single window environment as a "cross border, 'intelligent', facility that allows parties involved in trade and transport to lodge standardized information, mainly electronic, with a single entry point to fulfil all import, export and transit related regulatory requirements" (footnote 8, p. 4). The single window environment is achieved through collaboration between CBRAs and by the extensive use of information and communication technology (ICT). "Single window environment" describes the desirable interoperability between systems that will enable streamlined and automated processes. The single window system on its own, without interconnected CBRA systems, will not make trade processes significantly more efficient.

6   WTO. TFA Database. https://tfadatabase.org/information-for-traders/operation-of-the-single-window (accessed July 2021).
7   WCO. 2017. *Building a Single Window Environment*. Volume 1. Brussels.

As a result of the popularity and demand for the NSW, the term "single window" has been eagerly and loosely adopted for similar systems, at times commercially motivated. This has created so much confusion in the trade community that UN/CEFACT issued a technical note, *Terminology for Single Window and Other ePlatforms*.[8] To further minimize the misuse of the term "single window," UN/CEFACT updated the definition of the NSW in 2020.[9] The 2005 definition states: "A Single Window is defined as a facility that allows parties involved in trade and transport …" The 2020 definition was changed to "A Single Window is defined as a facility providing trade facilitation that allows parties involved in trade and transport…" The UN had to add "providing trade facilitation" to clarify the scope of the NSW and eliminate the misleading use of the term.

The NSW is continuously evolving. The complexity of implementation dictates gradual and progressive buildup of features. The NSW interfaces with stakeholder systems, which have their own separate programs of enhancements and budgets. The NSW evolves through different stages and its scope widens to bring in additional stakeholder groups and businesses. The United Nations Economic and Social Commission for Asia and the Pacific (UNESCAP) summarizes the NSW's evolution (Figure 3).[10] As the NSW matures, transactions can extend to include B2B exchanges. For example, Singapore's NSW, launched in 2019, supports simplified trade finance applications for leading trade finance banks. Users and banks benefit from improved efficiency and productivity.

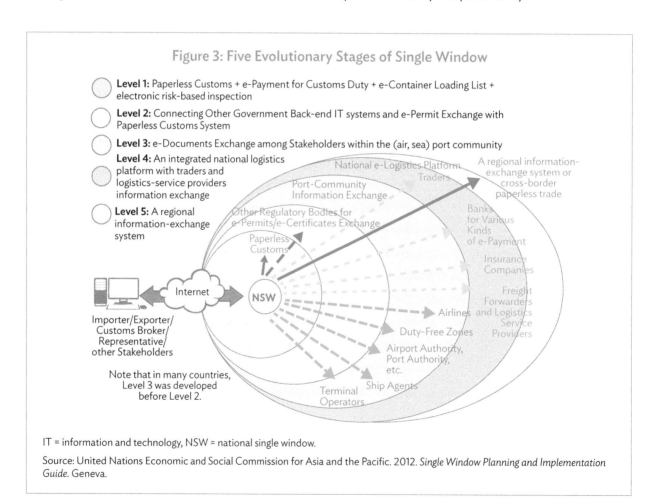

Figure 3: Five Evolutionary Stages of Single Window

Level 1: Paperless Customs + e-Payment for Customs Duty + e-Container Loading List + electronic risk-based inspection

Level 2: Connecting Other Government Back-end IT systems and e-Permit Exchange with Paperless Customs System

Level 3: e-Documents Exchange among Stakeholders within the (air, sea) port community

Level 4: An integrated national logistics platform with traders and logistics-service providers information exchange

Level 5: A regional information-exchange system

Note that in many countries, Level 3 was developed before Level 2.

IT = information and technology, NSW = national single window.

Source: United Nations Economic and Social Commission for Asia and the Pacific. 2012. *Single Window Planning and Implementation Guide*. Geneva.

8   UN/CEFACT. 2017. *Terminology for Single Window and Other ePlatforms, Version 1*. Geneva.
9   UN/CEFACT. 2020. *Recommendation No. 33. Recommendation and Guidelines on Establishing a Single Window*. Geneva.
10   UNESCAP. 2012. *Single Window Planning and Implementation Guide*. Bangkok.

The progression from levels 1 to 3—paperless customs, extension of interfaces to other CBRAs, and exchanges with airports and seaports—reflect the usual buildup of NSW features. In any specific country, the evolution may, however, include different feature sets and the sequence may not follow the same pattern. In some countries, the transport, logistics, and cargo communities may operate a system to facilitate information exchanges (B2B) between private sector stakeholders as well as with the authorities (B2G). For example, a port community system (PCS) may be established for ports, ship agents, freight forwarders, haulers, and other logistics service providers to exchange and process information on, for example, containerized and bulk cargo, tracking and tracing of cargo vessels, and dangerous goods. The NSW and PCS can exchange data, with regulatory approvals being transmitted to the PCS and cargo details and logistics information flowing to the NSW. The main interoperability implication will consist of data harmonization of the PCS with standards established by the NSW. System–to–system interoperability is not an issue since multiple options are available.

II

Why Implement the National Single Window?

CBRAs in many developing countries tend to have a strong silo culture and limited interagency collaboration. Border control procedures have been prepared with mostly paper-based and manual tools. Traders submit large volumes of information and documents to government authorities to comply with import, export, and transit regulations. Often the information and documentation must be duplicated and submitted to several agencies, each with its own manual or automated system and its own paper forms. The requirements, with associated compliance costs, burden governments and businesses. Traders are heavily penalized and face delayed clearance of goods and high costs. Such an environment for documentary and border control compliance is inefficient, resource-intensive, and time-consuming, and thus a major barrier to the growth of international trade. The problem of inefficient border control procedures is exacerbated by the increasing volume of trade. For example, exporting takes about 22 days in Southeast Asia and 29 days in South Asia, compared with the Organisation for Economic Co-operation and Development (OECD) average of fewer than 12 days.[11] OECD research estimates that Asia stands to reduce potential trade costs by 17.2% from trade facilitation reforms, and Europe and Central Asia could reduce costs by 14.8%.[12]

The NSW system provides a highly practical means of improving border clearance. The NSW's impact on streamlining and reducing time and cost of border control procedures is well-documented (footnote 11):

- After Singapore adopted the NSW, the time to process trade documents was reduced from 4 days to 15 minutes.
- Thailand trade facilitation measures using the NSW have eliminated redundant processes and reduced the number of days for export from 24 (in 2006) to 14 (in 2009).
- In Hong Kong, China, annual savings from the NSW are estimated at HK$1.3 billion.
- Total savings for the business community from the use of uTradeHub, which provides an automated information transaction system in the Republic of Korea, are estimated at $1.819 billion. Savings include those from transmission cost by using e-documents; expediting productivity by automating administrative work; and improving management, storage, and retrieval of information and documents by using information technology (IT).

The NSW serves as a "Trojan horse" to overcome institutional resistance to change and collaboration. International development organizations are, therefore, actively promoting and supporting NSW projects. The NSW is a win–win measure for all stakeholders involved in international trade and transport regulatory procedures. The WTO TFA, Article 10.4 provides clear direction for members in implementing the NSW.

---

[11]   United Nations Network of Experts for Paperless Trade and Transport in Asia and the Pacific (UNNExT). 2009. *Towards a Single Window Trading Environment. Brief.* 1. November. Bangkok.

[12]   OECD. 2018. *Trade Facilitation and the Global Economy.* Paris.

To appreciate the benefits of the NSW, it is useful to examine its base operational characteristics. Transactions are submitted to the NSW by any stakeholder, government, or private entity. The transactions are either keyed in or submitted as an electronic document from a stakeholder system. Once the NSW receives a transaction, the system automatically determines how to handle it. No intervention of NSW staff or management is required to process the transaction since the rules for processing each possible transaction are programmed in the NSW. The automated processing and/or information exchange are what constitute the NSW's tremendous capability. In addition to speed of processing, the automated feature also allows the NSW to operate 24 hours a day, 7 days a week, except during system maintenance, which typically lasts 2 or 3 hours. Error-handling procedures are built in to manage any abnormal transaction submitted.

Features and Benefits

NSW implementation usually includes the following:

- electronic submission of transactions (eliminating the need for physical submission of documents),
- automated processing of incoming transactions,
- automated sharing of documents and data with agreed parties,
- electronic receipt of communications from CBRAs,
- online support within the NSW for processing applications for permits (for CBRAs with no back-office permit-processing system),
- access to status of trader transactions, and
- electronic payment confirmation using a link to e-payment services.

With the features built into the NSW, each group of stakeholders derives benefits:

Traders

- time savings in submission of transactions
- cost savings as fewer resources are required to comply
- transparency of processing
- standardization and predictability of procedures
- tracking of status of transaction

Cargo Carriers and Cargo Handlers

- time savings
- cost savings
- elimination of errors in cargo status
- elimination of any insider fraudulent manipulation of information
- operational efficiency in discharge of pre-advised containers for inspection

Cross-Border Regulatory Agencies

- timely delivery of services
- improved coordination with other CBRAs, leading to better border control
- upgraded monitoring of service-level agreements (SLAs)
- greater efficiency from streamlined procedures and data harmonization

Women Entrepreneurs and Micro, Small, and Medium-Sized Enterprises

- an easily accessible environment where they can transact with minimal cost and without the need of intermediaries
- a neutral and women-friendly environment that eliminates potential gender discrimination from CBRAs

The combination of the NSW benefits reduces time and cost of trade transactions, leads to efficient and better border control, and contributes to the economy's competitiveness. Box 1 describes some of the benefits from Singapore's TradeNet.

Box 1: Benefits of TradeNet, Singapore's National Single Window

TradeNet reduced the processing time of typical trade documents from 2–4 days to as short as 15 minutes. Most transactions are completed in less than 10 minutes. Time savings have increased productivity. Studies suggest that TradeNet reduced trade documentation processing costs by 20% or more. Users of TradeNet found significant savings accruing from filling out a single online form now versus more than 20 paper forms in the past.

TradeNet streamlined trade procedures and protocols, which made the entire trading community more competitive internationally. The use of clerks or couriers to transport trade documents to various agencies was eliminated, saving time and improving deployment of staff and vehicles. Staff no longer needed to stand in queues and wait for documents to be cleared. Faster turnaround made it possible to better organize shipments and improve overall productivity. Freight forwarders have reported savings of 25%–35% in handling trade documentation as TradeNet operates 24 hours, unlike agencies that are open only during normal office hours.

Source: United Nations Network of Experts for Paperless Trade and Transport in Asia and the Pacific. 2010. Towards a Single Window Trading Environment Best Practice in Single Window Implementation: Case of Singapore's TradeNet. Brief No. 2. March.

The NSW catalyzes the rebooting of legal, regulatory, and administrative procedures and practices. For example, many CBRAs charge service fees. In many countries, NSWs have exerted pressure to make e-payment services available to avoid delays inherent in manual payment systems. Since similar end–to–end e-payment features are required by a multitude of other e-government services, the NSW catalyzes the emergence of such critical and crosscutting e-government support services.

The NSW is an example of a functional and beneficial system to improve delivery of government services. In several countries, the NSW operator has used its experience and, in some cases, its core infrastructure to implement other e-government services. CrimsonLogic in Singapore and Mauritius Network Services Ltd. are examples of NSW operators that have developed B2G services such as business registration, e-filing of pension contributions, pay-as-you-earn taxation, and e-judiciary.

The NSW has two features that benefit regional cooperation and integration:

(i)   Standardizing and simplifying border clearance procedures across the entire country, including remote border posts, and reducing the cost and complexity of dealing with multiple systems. Traders near subnational border areas are in a better position to operate and engage in cross-border trade.
(ii) Within the context of a subregional or larger regional trading agreement, single window international interoperability (SWII) will substantially benefit cross-border trade facilitation. ADB guides and supports member in planning, preparation, and implementation of NSWs, and will promote SWII to expedite regional cross-border trade.

III

Governance and Road Map for Designing the National Single Window

Although the concept is simple, establishing an NSW is not a "plug and play" activity, nor is it possible to simply replicate what has worked in one country into another country that has different capabilities, resources, and institutional problems.[13] Setting up an NSW is highly complex, and its many challenges concern not only technology but also

- political support and commitment,
- long-term commitment from top management,
- a reliable institutional platform for interagency collaboration,
- effective management of stakeholders' expectations and perceptions,
- workable business procedures,
- architectural models,
- data and business interoperability,
- laws and regulations, and
- financial issues.[14]

Setting the Stage

Given the complexity of implementing the NSW, a feasibility study is a common starting point to determine the NSW's potential scope, level and nature of demand, data and other information requirements, legal issues, potential benefits, options for implementation, cost estimates and implementation time frame, and implementation strategy. The approach follows the WCO phases to develop an NSW: agreement on the concept, feasibility study, and design and setup of the NSW environment.

The preparation and design of the NSW requires substantial effort to overcome resistance to change, deep-rooted practices, misconceptions of the NSW's role, and bureaucracies' inherent predisposition to protect existing responsibilities against perceived threats. The World Bank's International Trade Department summarizes the approach required: "Overcoming these challenges will require a stronger focus on developing broad-based commitment during project design, greater attention to identifying the individual accountabilities and goals of all participating agencies, longer time frames for implementation, and a good deal more face-to-face support during implementation."[15]

---

[13] G. McLinden. 2013. Single Window Systems: What We Have Learned. *World Bank Blogs*. 30 April. https://blogs.worldbank.org/trade/single-window-systems-what-we-have-learned.

[14] UNESCAP and UNECE. 2012. *Single Window Planning and Implementation Guide*. New York and Geneva. https://www.unescap.org/sites/default/files/0%20-%20Full%20Report_5.pdf.

[15] World Bank. 2012. Collaborative Border Management: A New Approach to an Old Problem. *Economic Premise*. 78. p. 5. https://openknowledge.worldbank.org/bitstream/handle/10986/10044/678690BRI00PUB00economic0premise078.pdf?sequence=1&isAllowed=y.

The NSW introduces changes to the established operating environment, which can be unsettling to government agency leaders who may be concerned about their roles, responsibilities, and authority. The standardization and transparency of NSW processes may be seen as a roadblock to rent seeking. It is not unusual for some CBRAs to express resistance to the NSW. Customs agencies, for example, sometimes misunderstand the role of the NSW and may be concerned about the dilution of their role in border control. Adequate preparation and resources are required to secure the buy-in of policy makers and key government agencies. On-site workshops delivered by experts can clarify that the NSW supports and upgrades border control procedures and does not dilute customs agencies' control. Sharing the experience of other NSWs with senior government officials has proven to be highly effective. Impromptu questions and concerns arise during workshops and candid interactions help deepen participants' understanding of the NSW and enlist participants' support. Getting buy-in should start from the concept phase and continue to feasibility and design, and should not be limited to government agencies but also include private sector associations of traders, transport, and logistics service providers. UNESCAP and the United Nations Network of Experts for Paperless Trade and Transport in Asia and the Pacific (UNNExT) offer workshops on implementing NSWs. Study tours of operational NSWs can provide insights on their operations and experience in implementation.

Governance of the National Single Window

An NSW project requires a governance structure to match and tackle the complex design steps that lie ahead. Sustainable institutional reform is complex enough when only one government agency is involved, but the risks and challenges multiply when many agencies are involved, as is the case for the NSW. The reform process associated with the NSW environment must, therefore, be supported by creating a governance structure that reinforces the different components of work required. Figure 4 shows a practical governance structure.

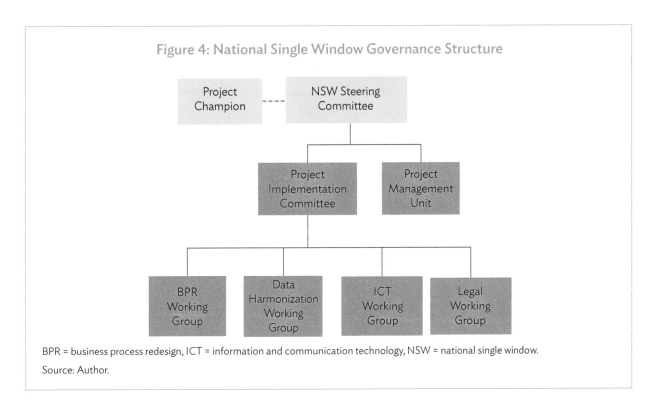

Figure 4: National Single Window Governance Structure

BPR = business process redesign, ICT = information and communication technology, NSW = national single window.

Source: Author.

National Single Window Steering Committee

The steering committee's key responsibilities include the following:

- Develop and set the NSW vision and goals.
- Protect the government's policy interests in the NSW.
- Decide on the NSW's scope and priorities.
- Ensure the active support and collaboration of ministries and government agencies.
- Provide policy oversight for the NSW operator.

The steering committee guides and directs CBRAs from different ministries. The appointment of the steering committee by the highest possible level of government boosts its role and authority. In Thailand, for example, the cabinet appointed a national committee on logistics development, whose members were permanent secretaries of economy-related ministries and representatives from trade-related associations. Such high-level commitment made stakeholders accountable to the project and obligated them to collaborate (footnote 11). International experience in implementing NSWs has shown that an NSW project champion is key. Setting up the NSW requires commitment, involvement, and coordinated action by many government ministries and agencies. A senior government official acting as an NSW project champion—preferably from the Prime Minister's office or ministries of finance or trade—would greatly benefit the project by securing collaboration across government ministries and agencies. The choice of the NSW project champion is a government decision. The champion helps ensure the continuity of commitment since the NSW project spans several years, during which officials may change. Box 2 describes examples of involvement of senior politicians as project champions. The Republic of Korea and Singapore demonstrate political commitment to all stakeholders and provide strong support for stakeholder coordination:[16]

- Political commitment has a direct bearing on resource mobilization. Establishing and maintaining an NSW demand significant resources. Usually, the stronger the political commitment, the more resources can be mobilized.
- Political commitment is required to engage stakeholders in implementing the NSW. Bringing in key players, particularly powerful government agencies, may be successful only if the project has political support at the top.
- Political commitment is required to introduce NSW legislation. The NSW implementing organization needs legal authority. The enabling legal environment for an NSW usually requires revised or new legal provisions.
- While commitment to implement an NSW usually comes from within a country, it may sometimes originate from outside as an international or regional agreement, which could elicit strong political commitment from within the country.

Active and continuous involvement of the private sector is essential to create an effective NSW. The private sector not only directly benefits from the NSW and provides much practical knowledge of the issues on the ground, business requirements, and practical solutions, but also adds significant value to any NSW project. The sector must remain continuously involved throughout the entire project life cycle, from concept, design, and implementation, to secure its buy-in and commitment. Representatives of private sector stakeholders—such as customs brokers, shipping agents, and freight forwarders—may participate in an advisory or other capacity in the NSW steering committee.

---

[16]   UNNExT. 2011. Towards a Single Window Trading Environment—Achieving Effective Stakeholder Involvement. *Brief No. 7*. September.

Box 2: Project Champions—the Republic of Korea and Singapore

In 2003, the Government of the Republic of Korea established the National e-Trade Committee for implementing a single window, with a direct mandate from the Prime Minister. The Prime Minister himself chaired the committee, enforced the participation of ministers, and invited the top management of industry federations and associations as members. In 2005, the government strengthened the committee's mandate by passing the Electronic Trade Facilitation Act. A multi-ministry administrative committee was created to coordinate all relevant government agencies. Specialized working groups were formed to determine the scope and objectives of the single window.

In 1986, to emphasize the Government of Singapore's commitment to the single window project, then Minister for Trade and Industry and now Prime Minister Lee Hsien Loong announced that TradeNet would be completed within 2 years. The announcement had the effect of speeding up the work of various committees and officials and gave the TradeNet team full authority and resources.

Sources: United Nations Network of Experts for Paperless Trade and Transport in Asia and the Pacific (UNNExT). 2011. Towards a Single Window Trading Environment—Achieving Effective Stakeholder Involvement. *Brief No. 7.* September; UNNExT. 2010. Towards a Single Window Trading Environment—Best Practice in Single Window Implementation: Case of Singapore's TradeNet. *Brief No. 2.* March.

Project management unit. While the NSW steering committee provides guidance, support, and oversight to the NSW project, a project management unit (PMU) is essential to coordinate and manage the activities of the many stakeholders. The NSW is complex and made up of multiple interrelated projects that must be executed concurrently. The PMU is responsible for planning and monitoring all activities related to implementing the NSW. The PMU does the following:

- Prepare the master plan for NSW implementation.
- Initiate road map of activities and monitor execution.
- Coordinate with CBRA project managers to ensure that the plan is followed.
- Prepare and execute an NSW communications plan.
- Tackle and resolve technical issues.
- Escalate issues to the NSW steering committee.
- Submit regular progress reports to the NSW steering committee.

The PMU is led by a full-time experienced project manager with overall responsibility for the timely execution of the NSW master plan. Given the nature of the NSW master plan activities, the PMU may include the following on a full-time basis:

- business analysts knowledgeable of international trade procedures,
- software engineers experienced in large software application systems and application interfaces, and
- an administrative assistant.

The PMU head is ideally appointed from a government organization. The PMU will extensively interact with CBRAs and other government organizations, and the government official must have experience dealing with such an environment. If such an official is not available, the PMU head can be sourced from the private sector. He or she must have a track record in project management and, preferably, experience in working on complex ICT projects. Business analysts should be highly knowledgeable of border control procedures and are usually appointed from a customs agency, port, airport, or ministry of trade. Software engineers can be selected from government organizations with in-house ICT departments. A customs agency is a likely source of such resources. Other options include national e-government organizations.

The PMU should be supported by an international expert with experience in designing an NSW and NSW road map of procurement components. The expert can guide and advise the PMU on executing the NSW master plan and participate in key reviews and key phases of the plan. The expert can regularly provide the NSW steering committee his or her independent assessment of the progress on executing the plan.

Project implementation committee. The project implementation committee's function is to provide technical direction and oversight during NSW development, implementation, and initial operations. The committee is responsible for approving, defining, and realizing benefits; monitoring risk; maintaining quality and the schedule; and escalating issues in any of these areas to the NSW steering committee.

The project implementation committee will do the following:

- Provide direction and oversight to the technical working groups, PMU, and users of the project outputs.
- Approve NSW project plans, scopes of work, deliverables, events, activities, timetables, staff resourcing, project expenditures, and project modifications.
- Reconcile differences in opinion and technical approach and resolve disputes arising from them.
- Ensure that the project's scope aligns with stakeholder groups' requirements.
- Report on project progress to the NSW steering committee.

The NSW involves many CBRAs, and one or two stakeholders should lead in promoting and coordinating the reform of border control procedures. The lead agency is usually customs or the ministry of trade and commerce, which both have a keen interest in trade facilitation. The port authority is actively involved since inefficient border procedures lead to congestion at ports. The customs office is frequently the lead agency given its wide-ranging responsibilities and presence across the entire territory. The lead agency chairs the project implementation committee. Its proposals are subject to CBRA legislation or regulations. The lead agency is distinct from the NSW operator, which is responsible for operating and maintaining the NSW system. The role of the lead agency spans from project initiation to design and procurement. The NSW operations may be assigned by policy makers to another organization or to the lead agency. The rules on the recommended approach are not set since policy makers decide based on conditions in the country. Examples of approach taken for the lead agency are provided in Box 3.

Box 3: Examples of Lead Agency

The customs agency is typically a strong candidate for the lead agency because of its inherent and substantial control over trade procedures and close interactions with other government agencies in international trade and border control. In several cases—e.g., Indonesia, Thailand, and Viet Nam—customs authorities led single window implementation.

Other agencies or different organizational arrangements may serve as the lead agency depending on national circumstances:

- Malaysia: Ministry of International Trade and Industry
- Singapore: Singapore Trade Development Board (renamed International Enterprise Singapore)
- Kenya: Kenya Revenue Authority and Kenya Ports Authority

Regardless of the lead agency, the customs authority should be included in single window implementation because it controls a large portion of trade procedures and border control measures.

Source: United Nations Network of Experts for Paperless Trade and Transport in Asia and the Pacific. 2011. Towards a Single Window Trading Environment—Achieving Effective Stakeholder Involvement. *Brief No. 7*. September.

The design and execution of the NSW master plan requires input from CBRAs and private sector stakeholders. Multiple tasks await each CBRA: input during business process redesign (BPR), assessment of changes brought about by BPR, implications of data harmonization, preparation of SLAs, and assessment of the impact of NSW operations on computer systems. All the tasks need to be coordinated within each CBRA, which should designate a project manager to participate in the steering committee.

Working groups. Implementing the NSW requires detailed review, analysis of issues, and potential solutions. The areas to be assessed are the following:

- BPR to streamline existing processes,
- data harmonization to standardize data definitions and formats,
- ICT interactions of existing systems with the NSW and expected NSW features, and
- legal assessment to identify legal amendments required for NSW implementation.

One working group is required for each area and will be made up of CBRA representatives, traders, cargo carriers, cargo operators, and the government.

Capacity-building program. A comprehensive capacity-building program is required to provide key skills needed to design the NSW and manage its preparation and implementation. A team of international experts and local CBRA staff will be required for the design components. CBRA staff are knowledgeable of local border control practices, and targeted capacity-building sessions will impart the complementary skills needed to enable them to contribute fully to NSW design. Capacity building should cover business process analysis, data harmonization, and the legal framework. In some cases, CBRA staff may require basic IT skills training if they have been operating in a paper-based, manual environment before interfacing with the NSW. NSW design and implementation are highly complex and require coordinated activities across many organizations. Project management and change management for CBRA project managers and the PMU are highly recommended. A project management methodology for the NSW should be agreed on. The methodology can be adopted from the Project Management Institute's *A Guide to the Project Management Body of Knowledge* or Projects in Controlled Environments. Alternately, a simplified methodology can be agreed on that includes the key processes of project planning, project control, change control, and project closeout. UNNExT is a potential resource for capacity building on these and other NSW-related themes. Up-front planning is required to match delivery of capacity building in time for the work to be carried out. The capacity-building program needs to include private sector contributions to the NSW during the test phases and change management sessions to prepare private sector stakeholders for the NSW environment.

Road Map for National Single Window Design Components

Designing the NSW is complex and involves five major components. The design's complexity arises from the need to establish the flow of information and integration of border control processes across all stakeholders within the NSW environment. The components support fundamental pillars that must be aligned for a properly functioning NSW. The United Nations Conference on Trade and Development (UNCTAD) has issued recommendations on three of the components: business process analysis and BPR, data harmonization, and legal framework. The SLA is an essential component since it captures one of the NSW's main objectives: the formal commitment of the CBRA on measurable indicators of service delivery. Finally, the technical design of the NSW environment is the fifth component, translating the business process requirements into a technical design and interfaces between the NSW and other stakeholder systems.

Policy decisions are required to establish the governance structure, set the vision and goals of the NSW, and the NSW business model. Technical work needs to deal with (i) BPR; (ii) targets for improved delivery of CBRA services; (iii) standardization of data definitions to enable data sharing and reuse; (iv) interoperability of the NSW, the CBRA, and other stakeholder systems; and (v) an enabling legal framework to support changes resulting from the NSW. Completing the technical design components paves the way to preparing detailed requirement specifications for procurement of the NSW system and enhancements for stakeholder systems to interoperate with the NSW. The road map (Figure 5) depicts the relationship of policy decisions and the sequence of technical design components that lead to the specifications for implementation. This road map captures the main outputs that lay the ground for NSW implementation.

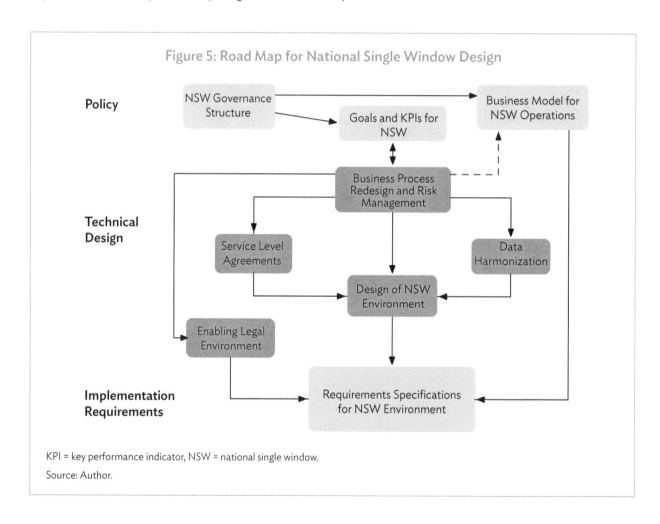

Figure 5: Road Map for National Single Window Design

KPI = key performance indicator, NSW = national single window.
Source: Author.

Goals and Key Performance Indicators

Setting goals and key performance indicators (KPIs) for the NSW is a powerful approach to mobilize public and private sector stakeholders. The KPIs clarify the targets and guide technical design decisions. The choice of goals and indicators are determined by policy makers. Performance indicators such as those available from UNCTAD and the Central Asia Regional Economic Cooperation Program's corridor performance measurement and monitoring can be a benchmark; the target is improvement once the NSW operates. Another approach is reducing time for import and export procedures. As the NSW design progresses, the project team provides the findings to policy makers, who may further refine the goals and KPIs. The NSW provides the capability, previously unavailable, to monitor the performance of each CBRA in border control.

Business Process Redesign and Risk Management

The NSW can deliver streamlined services to trade and transport stakeholders simply and efficiently. However, the possible benefits to the NSW are not achieved by simply automating existing procedures. Instead, they need to be analyzed, assessed, and redesigned considering, where relevant, the possibilities offered by the NSW environment and current data communications and electronic interchange to streamline procedures.

The BPR methodology consists of the analysis of existing "as is" processes to identify inefficiencies and redesign of "to be" processes between stakeholders and within stakeholder organizations. The "as is" review examines in detail each activity to identify redundancies and non–value-added activities in procedural and documentary requirements as well as outdated laws or unnecessary regulations. Once a consensus is reached on improvements, "to be" processes are defined to eliminate bottlenecks and inefficiencies of procedures and documentary requirements in the examined business process. Examples of recommendations include (i) merging some procedures, (ii) eliminating redundant procedures and unnecessary documentary requirements, (iii) automating procedures to promote sharing trade and transport data among stakeholders, and (iv) modifying related laws and regulations to facilitate the operation of the newly designed business processes.[17]

CBRAs in developing countries do not have the same levels of service computerization. Customs will usually have an advanced computer system while other CBRAs may be operating in a manual environment. The NSW can cater to CBRAs that have not yet computerized their services by offering features within the NSW system for the CBRAs to sign into the NSW to receive applications for licenses, permits, certificates, and others (LPCOs) and respond to applications. The sophistication and complexity of the features provided by the NSW for CBRAs are determined by volume of transactions, critical nature of LPCOs, budget, and schedule. CBRAs interacting with the NSW require computers and data communications to link to the NSW. As for CBRAs with an in-house system, information exchanges with the NSW and processing of information are determined by the BPR review.

In some cases, border control procedures may become unnecessary. LPCOs that were mandated years ago or components of control that have become irrelevant can be eliminated. For example, after the BPR study in 2017, the Maldives Ministry of Economic Development acknowledged that import and export licenses were no longer relevant.[18] The licenses originated from a law enacted in 1979. Eliminating an LPCO is the ultimate process simplification. BPRs also often result in identification of quick wins, i.e., improvements that can be made rapidly without the NSW.

The NSW environment consists of the new NSW system and interfaces to existing systems such as the customs management system (CMS), the business registration system at the ministry of trade, and other CBRA systems. In some countries, the systems may be mature and already provide online access. If so, the NSW design may need to consider a progressive approach to implementing a single entry point since changing the end-user interface, for example, from the CMS to the NSW can imply major changes. The issue is not simply enabling data capture but

[17]   UNECE. 2011. *Single Window Implementation Framework*. Geneva and New York. https://unece.org/fileadmin/DAM/cefact/publica/ SWImplementationFramework.pdf.

[18]   ADB. 2019. *Potential Exports and Nontariff Barriers to Trade—Maldives National Study*. Manila.

building a complex set of data validation and business-processing rules into the CMS. When the NSW and the CMS (or other CBRA system) are implemented at the same time, their design and interfaces are simplified since the existing CMS does not impose any constraint. In such cases, implementing the single entry point is easier.

Risk management allows CBRAs to facilitate trade by focusing their intervention on high-risk items and allowing for more streamlined procedures for lower-risk ones. Risk management thus enables better utilization of limited resources. Most customs organizations have already embarked on risk management with functionality built into their procedures and their CMS. Fewer CBRAs have adopted risk management as part of their border control procedures. The NSW provides an opportunity to implement a risk management engine, where each CBRA has independent risk parameter settings. The NSW can be configured to alert the CBRA once a customs declaration has been submitted. Customs risk management continues to operate within the CMS. The International Organization for Standardization (ISO) 31000:2009 provides a general risk management model that can be considered by CBRAs. A risk management approach is carried out as part of the BPR since the business processes related to risk management have an impact on process flows. For example, once a risk has been detected by the ministry of health, events such as notification to customs, joint inspection, and results of inspection must be agreed upon. The decisions influence the business processes and must be agreed upon during the BPR review. WCO's Building a Single Window Environment includes a case study by Mauritius customs of implementing a two-tier risk management approach within the NSW and in the CMS.[19]

The BPR is a key creative design component that defines the streamlined operations of the NSW environment. The BPR output establishes the changes for simplified procedures, service improvements, better border controls, and interoperability of NSW and CBRA systems. The changes serve as input to the subsequent design components of SLAs, data harmonization, and design of the NSW environment. Process changes identified by the BPR may also lead to amendments to the legal framework. Once the BPR is completed, the portrayal of the future operating environment for international trade procedures may influence policy decisions on the business model to be adopted for the NSW operator.

Adequate resources and time must be allocated for a comprehensive BPR to ensure high-impact trade facilitation outcomes. The BPR working group should include representatives from CBRAs and the private sector who have deep knowledge of the processes. A keen sense of the possibilities of ICT will add value. UNESCAP has prepared a guide to which the BPR working group can refer.[20] An experienced international consultant should be recruited to provide insight on how the NSW can implement key trade facilitation features such as coordinated border management as recommended by WCO and WTO TFA, Article 8; streamlined processes with cargo carriers and cargo handlers; and e-payment integration from trader instruction to automated confirmation of receipt by the CBRA bank.[21] The BPR lasts 4–6 months depending on the country's circumstances.

Box 4 provides details of changes to procedures for processing trade documents in Singapore as a result of TradeNet implementation.

[19]   WCO. 2017. *Building a Single Window Environment—Integrated Risk Management.* Part VIII, Volume 2. Brussels.
[20]   UNESCAP. 2009. *Business Process Analysis Guide to Simplify Trade Procedures.* Bangkok.
[21]   WCO. 2018. *Coordinated Border Management.* Brussels.

Box 4: Business Process Redesign in Singapore—TradeNet

The table highlights differences in trade administration before and after TradeNet implementation. Trade declaration documents submitted through TradeNet need not have supporting documents (e.g., invoices and bills of lading). The Trade Development Board places the onus on the traders to honestly and accurately report information. However, to prevent abuse, Trade Development Board randomly checks on traders by requiring them to forward supporting documents within 48 hours of approval of their declaration documents. Heavy penalties are imposed on offenders who provide false information. As a senior trade documentation manager explained, "We had to do away with the need for supporting documents. We didn't want to overlay the old way of doing things onto the automated system. We won't gain any leverage from the system that way. Faced with scarcity of labor and a government cap on manpower increases in the civil service, we decided to create a compromised system of trust which lets the horses run through the gate but reins them later when necessary."

Feature	Pre-TradeNet	Post-TradeNet
Trade documents	Multiple copies	Single copies
Supporting documents	Required	Only for random checks
Counter clerks	Process all documents	Process few documents
Serving counters	More than 20	Fewer than 5
Supervisors	Batch documents	Step eliminated
Data entry clerks	Key data for documents	Step eliminated
Document validation	Manual	Automated
Feedback provision	Phone, mail	Electronic messages
Document approval	Documents with permit numbers	Electronic messages with permit numbers
Office attendants	Handle document submission and distribution	Step eliminated
Distribution mailboxes	One per trader	Electronic mailboxes
Fee collection • Document processing • Custom duties • Network usage	Revenue stamps Checks Not applicable	Bank account deduction Bank account deduction Bank account deduction

Source: H. Teo, B. Tan, and K. Wei. 1997. Organizational Transformation Using Electronic Data Interchange: The Case of TradeNet in Singapore. *Journal of Management Information Systems*. 13 (4).

Service-Level Agreements

Timeliness and predictability of services are key to ease of doing business. CBRAs are expected to respond within an acceptable time frame to requests, applications, and declarations from importers and exporters. The BPR output for international trade flows includes agreed performance targets at each step of the process chain once the NSW is operational. Within one process chain, e.g., import, one or more CBRAs are involved. Each is expected to deliver its specific service within an agreed time frame.

In line with international good practice, CBRA targets and commitments to achieve them need to be captured in an SLA. The NSW operator is expected to deliver services and perform at a certain level. The SLA specifies the obligations of each agency, the expected service level, support and escalation procedures, contact details, among others. The SLA should incorporate an end-user usage agreement that clarifies the rights and obligations of the registered traders and stakeholders. The NSW can monitor the performance of the CBRA against its SLA and report in real time to staff and management. SLAs help set clear targets and factual feedback from the NSW informs management of performance, issues to be resolved, and response to improvement measures taken.

The NSW operator must commit to an SLA. The NSW steering committee is expected to provide policy guidelines that set NSW operator commitments and obligations to provide and meet pre-agreed service levels, including specified NSW functions. To achieve the intended outcomes, SLAs need to be monitored. The NSW needs to incorporate a monitoring framework that allows drawing up SLAs for each CBRA; identifying and recording data required to measure service levels; and eventual tracking, monitoring, and reporting service levels by the NSW. The monitoring of services delivered enables prompt identification of bottlenecks and corrective measures to be determined by management.

Data Harmonization

The single window concept is premised on efficient data exchange between traders, transport service providers, and CBRAs. Semantic differences in data collected between CBRAs are common; for example, one CBRA may provide three data fields for addresses while another one may use four. Dissimilar data structures that have been exchanged automatically cannot be reconciled automatically. Semantic interoperability of data must be resolved to enable efficient and smooth interoperability of the systems within the NSW environment. Harmonizing data used in trade documents and aligning them with international standards ensure data interoperability among the parties engaged in a trade transaction. Data harmonization is a prerequisite for the NSW to share data and for recipient systems to automatically process the data.

Various data standards have evolved over the years to standardize trade data and procedures. However, the recent trend among customs and other authorities is to adopt the WCO data model as their reference to benefit from the following:

- The data dictionary is comprehensive and provides all CBRAs with a common operational vocabulary, language, and syntax.
- The model fosters coordinated border management.
- As a global standard, trade documents are easier to exchange as regional and international interoperability emerges with other NSW systems.
- The model supports the exchange of electronic documents in standard United Nations/Electronic Data Interchange for Administration, Commerce and Transport (UN/EDIFACT) or extensible markup language (XML) syntax.

At the country level, one common issue is the lack of a standard personal or corporate identification scheme used by stakeholders, including government agencies. For example, customs may use a tax account number (TAN) when a declaration is submitted, the ministry of trade may use a business registration number (BRN) when a permit is issued, and the container terminal number may use a client number for customs brokers and freight forwarders. The difficulty arises in determining that a TAN relates to the same business entity identified by a BRN or a client number. Each country needs to decide to either standardize identification schemes or implement a mapping mechanism where, for example, one TAN is equivalent to a BRN. Since 2009, Singapore, for example, has issued a unique number to all entities registered in Singapore, including businesses, local companies, limited liability partnerships, societies, health-care institutions, and trade unions. The entity number is permanent and cannot be changed even if the business name changes. The adoption of the global legal entity identifier, as promoted by the Global Legal Entity Identifier Foundation, is an option that government and financial regulators may consider.

The methodology for data harmonization is well-documented. The United Nations Economic Commission for Europe (UNECE) has published Recommendation No. 34, and WCO has prepared a guide covering the WCO data model and steps for single window data harmonization.[22] UNESCAP has prepared a similar guide that uses the term "single window environment."[23] The UN/CEFACT reference data model is the common basis for standardizing data.[24]

Design of the National Single Window Environment

The NSW expedites submission of data from traders and other stakeholders and enables collaboration between CBRAs through built-in processes and automated exchanges with stakeholders. After the BPR, all stakeholders agree on how the procedures are to be streamlined by (i) the NSW and its interactions with stakeholder systems and (ii) changes carried out within stakeholder systems. These features, together with the definition of SLAs and data harmonization outputs, are the basis for documenting the design of the multisystem NSW environment. The components of the design usually include the following:

(i)   interactions of NSW with
    (a) traders,
    (b) cargo carriers and cargo handlers,
    (c) customs management system,
    (d) CBRA systems,
    (e) national e-payment services,
    (f) coordinated border management,
    (g) management of SLAs, and
    (h) payment-related services and interface with national e-payment service;

(ii)   collaboration features to support facilitation mechanisms such as coordinated border management between CBRAs, from the issuance of LPCOs to declaration, inspection, and final cargo release;
(iii) extensive and fully documented interactions between NSW and customs;
(iv) risk management features for CBRAs and interactions with the customs system;
(v)   support such as workflow management for CBRAs that do not have back-end systems to control application processing;
(vi) management of SLAs to track CBRA and NSW performance and tracking and monitoring of SLAs to ensure good NSW governance; and
(vii) high-level description of changes to each stakeholder system to implement the BPR processes agreed upon and documentation of interactions and data exchanges agreed upon with the NSW.

---

[22] UNECE. 2013. *Recommendation No. 34. Data Simplification and Standardization for International Trade.* Geneva; and WCO. 2007. *Data Model. Single Window Data Harmonization.* Brussels.
[23] UNESCAP. 2012. *Data Harmonization and Modeling Guide for Single Window Environment.* Bangkok.
[24] UN/CEFACT. 2018. Reference Data Model. *White Paper.*

The ICT working group designs the NSW environment. The group includes representatives from CBRAs and private sector stakeholders familiar with the computer systems in their organizations. Business analysts from the BPR working group are involved to ensure that the design includes streamlined features from the BPR. The NSW environment design document should reinforce that NSW implementation consists not only of the NSW system but also associated changes to other systems and procedures that make up the entire NSW environment.

Enabling Legal Environment

Establishing an NSW shifts trade transactions to an electronic environment where applications, LPCOs, and other documents evolve from paper to electronic formats. The NSW operating environment will likely introduce many legal issues that will require changes to legislation and regulations, for example, laws on electronic submission of documents; electronic signatures, including digital signatures; user and message authentication; data sharing; data retention, destruction, and archiving; and electronic evidence.[25] The BPR outcome may change border control procedures and/or documents mandated in laws or regulations. Beyond national exchanges, provision for cross-border transactions is important as the benefits from NSW and related paperless trade systems would be greatly improved if the electronic documents they generate could be used across borders.

The mandate for the legal working group is to assess the legislative framework to determine the country's readiness to implement an NSW, including recommendations to harmonize legislation with international standards. The review can be guided by UN/CEFACT Recommendation No. 35, which provides a checklist for countries to assess their legal readiness to implement an NSW.[26] The UN legal codification work in electronic commerce, undertaken by the UN Commission on International Trade Law, can be considered the benchmark for developing the NSW legal infrastructure for national and international transactions.

At the institutional level, a memorandum of understanding (MOU) is required between the NSW operator and each stakeholder organization in the NSW environment. The NSW offers online services, exchanges data, and stores data from the CBRAs and cargo handlers, among others. An MOU is required between the NSW operator and each stakeholder to ensure that the agreement on interactions between the two parties are clear and data exchanged are protected. Fees, if applicable, are covered in the MOU.

Business Model for National Single Window Operations

Policy makers need to decide the business model for the entity responsible for NSW operations. The key considerations include governance of the NSW operator, type of structure most likely to deliver, and sustainability. The NSW is a highly visible collaboration by government agencies to deliver a critical government service to enable efficient trade. A clear governance mechanism is needed to do the following:

- Provide policy oversight.
- Oversee the success of the NSW in meeting government policy objectives.
- Protect the government's policy interests.
- Establish representation of CBRAs, traders, and logistics operators.

---

[25]   UNESCAP. 2012. *Electronic Single Window Legal Issues—A Capacity Building Guide.* Bangkok.
[26]   UN/CEFACT. 2010. *Recommendation No. 35. Establishing a Legal Framework for the International Trade Single Window.* Geneva.

Business model options include government agency, state-owned enterprise, and public–private partnership. There is no common or recommended model for the NSW operator. Each country has a unique context, cooperation mechanisms with the private sector, and governance structure, which determine the model selected. In choosing the model, the following should be considered:

- What is the likely performance and reliability of services of the operator model?
- To what degree does the operator model ease access to skills and technologies and enable hiring and firing; and buying, acquiring, and retiring technology?
- How agile (responsive to internal or external shocks and opportunities) is the operator under the model?
- To what degree does the operator model support access to finance required to establish, operate, and maintain the NSW?
- Does the operator model foster innovation?
- What is the cost or ease of establishing the operator model?

Key lessons learned point to the need to provide maximum operational flexibility, government control, a neutral setting, and involvement of private sector associations that convey business requirements and the operational realities on the ground. The business model must attract and retain qualified management and technical professionals.

The cost of an NSW system varies widely depending on countries' circumstances: design features, interfaces required with other stakeholder systems, reuse of existing software, hardware, infrastructure, among others. UN/CEFACT data indicate that "costs were less than $1 million in Guatemala, ranged between $1 million and $4 million in Finland, Germany, Senegal, Malaysia, and were significantly higher in countries such as the Republic of Korea (around $5 million in customs and $8 million in trade network), Ghana and Singapore, where the systems are quite extensive and cover many additional areas.[27]

The sustainability of the NSW operator is a key decision associated with the business model. The government needs to decide whether NSW services are free or not, with or without any government subsidy. If fees are payable, the government must define a user fee structure in consultation with government agencies and other stakeholders, including from the private sector. International experience should be considered along with WTO rules and other rules likely to emerge. The user fee is expected to cover at least the costs of operation and maintenance and future enhancements to the NSW. The preparation of a preliminary financial model, as part of the NSW feasibility study, has proven useful in helping the government decide on sustainability.

A UNESCAP study shows that NSW operations in 10 countries in Asia and the Pacific follow a mix of models, with no specific trend emerging.[28] WCO provides three examples of public–private partnership NSWs: TradeNet in Singapore, Nippon Airport Cargo Community System in Japan, and Mauritius Network Services (Table 1).[29] NSW implementation is relevant within broader trade facilitation initiatives. Box 5 describes Tunisia's experience in implementing the World Bank–funded Export Development project. Box 6 provides some additional examples of the diversity of single window models.

27 UN/CEFACT. 2011. *UNECE Single Window Repository.* Part 1.
28 UNESCAP. 2018. *Single Window for Trade Facilitation: Regional Best Practices and Future Development.* Bangkok.
29 WCO. 2017. *Building a Single Window Environment.* Volume 2. Brussels.

National Single Window Operator Model and Sustainability

Region	Member State	Operation Model	Main Operation Body	Main Source of Operation Budget
Central Asia	Armenia	Public	Customs	Government grants
Central Asia	Azerbaijan	Public	Customs	Government grants
Central Asia	Kyrgyz Republic	Public	Public Company	Government grants
Northeast Asia	Japan	PPP	Third-party SP	Commercial
Northeast Asia	Republic of Korea (UNIPASS)	Public	Customs	Government grant + Commercial
Northeast Asia	Republic of Korea (uTradeHub)	PPP	Third-party SP	Commercial
Pacific	New Zealand	Public	Customs	Government grants
Southeast Asia	Indonesia	Public	Public Company	Government grants
Southeast Asia	Malaysia	PPP	Third-party SP	Commercial
Southeast Asia	Singapore	PPP	Third-party SP	Commercial
Southeast Asia	Thailand	PPP	Customs	Government grant + Commercial

PPP = public–private partnership, SP = service provider.

Source: UNESCAP. 2018. *Single Window for Trade Facilitation: Regional Best Practices and Future Development.* Bangkok.

Box 5: Tunisia Trade Facilitation—World Bank

The major objective of the Tunisia Export Development project, funded by the World Bank, was to increase the ability of private exporters to integrate into the global economy. The trade facilitation component (International Bank for Reconstruction and Development financing of $15.3 million) had two subcomponents: (i) modernization of the customs information system and (ii) simplification of trade documents and clearance processes. The second subcomponent started streamlining trade clearance processes by simplifying trade documents (single administrative document) and automating processing (single window) to improve the efficiency of information exchange associated with cargo-handling and clearance activities through the use of information and communication technology (ICT). Tunisie Tradenet (TTN), a public–private company, was created to operate an automated network and develop end-user interfaces among key agencies involved in trade transaction clearance.

Outcome and Achievement of the Objective
Imported goods can now be cleared in 3 days on average, compared with 8 days on average at the time of project appraisal, making enterprises more competitive and market-responsive. Trade transactions are more efficient today than 5 years ago. Customs clearance time, for example, is 10 minutes for a declaration not requiring technical control, as opposed to 3 days in 2000.

The modernized customs agency is now more focused on trade facilitation than control. The simplified, automated processing of trade documents has had indirect effects on back-office reengineering and made border control agencies more efficient and trade clearance processes less time-consuming. The TTN is considered one of the most innovative trade documentation processing schemes in the region. Several other countries are implementing single windows for trade transactions based on the TTN's experience. (TTN won the Technology in Government in Africa award for delivery of online trade procedures in 2009 from the United Nations Economic Commission for Africa.)

continued on next page

Box 5: *continued*

Lessons Learned

The success of the project depends on strong government commitment. Tunisia's experience points to the dramatic institutional change that can be achieved through such an operation and to improvements in trade clearing that can result when administrative and political commitment combines with advances in ICT. Perhaps the most important prerequisite for success is commitment at the highest level of government. Such commitment was made possible by the close involvement of the minister of commerce and the supervision of the President, who also chaired the Superior Export and Investment Council, a cross-ministerial committee.

Other success factors included (i) simplifying customs requirements, (ii) extending electronic processing to all import and export administration and other agencies involved in trade transactions and developing their "back offices" to handle electronic processing of trade documents, (iii) adopting internationally recognized standards, and (iv) aligning the relative costs of processing documentation on paper and online.

Sources: World Bank. 2005. Implementation Completion Report (SCL-44750 TF-25327); Tunisia Export Development Project, Report 31785. Washington, DC.

Box 6: Diversity of Models

No unique model exists for a single window as operators adapt their systems to domestic and regional conditions and requirements.

Financing can be provided by the state (e.g., Azerbaijan, Finland, Macedonia, the Philippines, the Republic of Korea, Sweden, the United States); by the private sector (e.g., Germany, Guatemala); or with the help of a public–private partnership (e.g., Ghana; Hong Kong, China; Japan; Malaysia; Mauritius; Senegal; Singapore).

The use of single window facilities can be compulsory (Finland, Ghana, Guatemala, Mauritius, the Republic of Korea, Senegal) or voluntary (Germany; Hong Kong, China; Japan; Malaysia; Sweden; the United States).

Services vary and may be provided free of charge (Azerbaijan, Finland, Sweden, the United States) or based on various payment schemes (Germany; Ghana; Guatemala; Hong Kong, China; Japan; Malaysia; Mauritius; Senegal; Singapore). Even within one jurisdiction, a system can vary; in the Republic of Korea, for example, a single window facility run by the customs agency is free of charge and the Korea Trade Network single window charges fees.

Despite these differences, all participating economies speak favorably of their single window experience. The benefits and revenues generally outweigh the establishment and operational costs.

Source: United Nations Centre for Trade Facilitation and Electronic Business (UN/CEFACT). 2011. *United Nations Economic Commission for Europe (UNECE) Single Window Repository.* Part 1.

IV Implications of National Single Window Interoperability

Single window international interoperability (SWII) evolved from the NSW and has recently gained increasing attention. The Framework Agreement on Facilitation of Cross-Border Paperless Trade in Asia and the Pacific came into effect in February 2021. It aims to enable the exchange and mutual recognition of trade-related data and documents in electronic form and facilitate interoperability among national and subregional single windows or other paperless trade systems. The main business drivers are the following:

- regional integration to promote regional growth by simplifying, modernizing, and harmonizing export and import processes;
- trade facilitation to allow economic operators, including small and medium-sized companies, to comply with regulatory requirements to become more competitive in a global market;
- combating of illicit activities by forewarning the importing economy to ensure that merchandise is appropriately inspected;
- advanced security declarations to reinforce the principle of risk management by assessing the quality of data and act upon it as required; and
- risk analysis to allow government agencies in the importing economy to assess any security, safety, fiscal, or other risks in advance.

A number of SWII agreements are operational and they are mostly in Asia and the Pacific. These are:

- Association of Southeast Asian Nations (ASEAN) Single Window (ASW):
  » preferential certificates of origin, ASEAN customs declaration documents;
  » electronic exchange of certificates of origin between the 10 member countries since 2019; and
  » ASEAN customs declaration documents adopted by five countries since 2020.

- Pacific Alliance:
  » Chile, Republic of Colombia, Mexico, Peru launched SWII launched 2016;
  » sanitary and phytosanitary certificates (2017), certificates of origin (2018).

- Northeast Asia Logistics Information Service Network:
  » Sharing of vessel and container status: Japan, the People's Republic of China, the Republic of Korea.

- Australia and New Zealand system-level exchanges (not an NSW):
  » Exchange of sanitary and phytosanitary certificates between the Australian Quarantine and Inspection Service and the New Zealand Food Safety Authority.

The ASW Agreement was signed in 2005 and started operating in 2018. The ASW central server alone is responsible for managing the communication hub linking each ASEAN member state NSW. The ASW server does not retain, propagate, or archive any trade or regulatory information. The Pacific Alliance model is simpler and does not require any central server (or regional single window).[30] Member countries' NSWs operate an interoperability pack that allows electronic documents to be sent directly to another member country. The Pacific Alliance advanced its SWII in a short time. The Presidents of the four member countries signed an agreement in 2015 to make their NSWs interoperable to expedite inter-bloc trade. In 2017, the Pacific Alliance countries began exchanging phytosanitary certificate data in 2017 and certificate of origin data in 2018.

The Asia-Pacific Economic Cooperation 2018 study states that the active support of the Inter-American Development Bank (IDB) regional forum for dialogue and cooperation contributed to the Pacific Alliance's rapid progress. The forum, Inter-American Network of International Trade Single Windows (RedVUCE), catalyzes regional integration.[31] RedVUCE brings together public agencies and the private sector to design, develop, and administer single window systems for foreign trade in the Americas. During an online meeting in August 2021, IDB said that its support included (i) the supply and maintenance of software for SWII and (ii) two full-time consultants to assist the four member countries with their NSW and interoperability issues. IDB is considering approaches to sustainability. Member countries do not pay fees for SWII support.

The European Union has established the European Interoperability Framework (EIF) to provide guidance on national interoperability frameworks and to foster cross-border interoperability. The EIF maps out fundamental components of interoperability in four layers (Figure 6). The organizational interoperability layer refers to alignment of business processes to manage information exchanges and to provide services that meet the business community's requirements. Semantic interoperability refers to shared meaning of data elements, their relationships, and the syntax to enable data exchanges.

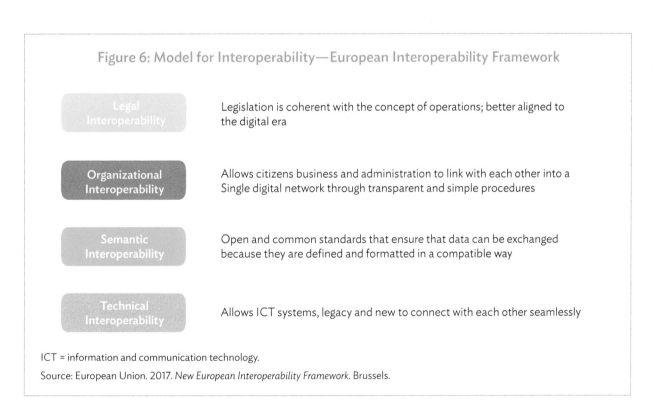

Figure 6: Model for Interoperability—European Interoperability Framework

Legal Interoperability	Legislation is coherent with the concept of operations; better aligned to the digital era
Organizational Interoperability	Allows citizens business and administration to link with each other into a Single digital network through transparent and simple procedures
Semantic Interoperability	Open and common standards that ensure that data can be exchanged because they are defined and formatted in a compatible way
Technical Interoperability	Allows ICT systems, legacy and new to connect with each other seamlessly

ICT = information and communication technology.

Source: European Union. 2017. *New European Interoperability Framework*. Brussels.

---

[30] Asia-Pacific Economic Cooperation Policy Support Unit. 2018. *Study on Single Window Systems International Interoperability*. Singapore.

[31] IDB. What is RedVUCE? https://redvuce.org/en/what-is-redvuce/.

The main issues in setting up SWII are (i) lack of data harmonization and adequate laws and regulations on (a) cross-border legal recognition of electronic data, (b) protection of commercial information, and (c) data retention and archiving; and (ii) difficulties in establishing an effective governance structure. The ASW experience provides useful lessons on SWII.[32] The essential components of SWII include the following:

(i)   Clear, ambitious, and feasible vision from senior officials, informed by the private sector, of what the regional mechanism must accomplish. A regional single window system for processing all forms for all countries in a region may not be a reasonable objective.

(ii)   An institutional setup where officials can come together to discuss and agree on features and technical and legal matters. The ASEAN Secretariat has played a critical role in coordinating the working groups and supporting the steering committee.

(iii) Regional legal impediments should be reviewed as early as possible. For example, the ASEAN Trade in Goods Agreement certificate of origin form D was mandated as a hard-copy document with a manual signature and the new electronic environment would conflict with this mandate.

(iv)   NSWs need to be substantially under way—if not in place—by the time discussions start on a regional mechanism to exchange data between them.

National implications of single window international interoperability. For countries that develop their NSW where SWII is a requirement, NSW design must comply with the preestablished interoperability requirements. The NSW components impacted are data harmonization, legal framework, and technical system interface. For countries without SWII requirements, adopting international standards such as the WCO data model likely minimizes the need for modifications when cross-border data exchange is eventually needed. When such requirements arise, partner countries negotiate data standards and legal and technical interface requirements. Once agreed upon, data definitions and system enhancements need to be changed to comply with standards and technical requirements to enable cross-border data exchange.

V Good Practice and Risk Mitigation

This section covers practices and approaches that contribute to successful preparation, design, and implementation of the NSW environment.

Experienced project management is essential. NSW implementation consists of not one project but multiple interrelated projects executed by many CBRAs, container terminals, airport cargo handlers, and others. Most challenges are not from technology but from getting individual agencies to collaborate to achieve a collective goal. The project management unit (PMU) head needs a broad set of project management and leadership skills and experience to validate project plans, secure the support of CBRA project managers and other decision makers, and ensure the coordination and synchronization of activities.

Capacity-building program. The program is required to provide key skills in design and management of NSW preparation and implementation. Project management and change management for CBRA project managers and the PMU are highly recommended. Agreeing on an NSW project management methodology would be useful. It can be adopted from the Project Management Institute's *A Guide to the Project Management Body of Knowledge* or Projects in Controlled Environments methodologies. Or a simplified methodology that includes the key processes of project planning, project control, change control, and project closeout can be agreed on. Project implementation team members should build their capacity to analyze business processes, harmonize data, and reform the legal framework. The UN Network of Experts for Paperless Trade and Transport in Asia and the Pacific (UNNeXT) is a potential resource for capacity-building sessions on these and other single window-related themes. Up-front planning is required to match delivery of capacity building in time for the work to be carried out.

Project charter. It is a key document that commits CBRAs and other stakeholder organizations to their NSW project deliverables. Once the design is completed, each CBRA prepares its project charter to confirm that it will operate as per the agreed streamlined business processes and data harmonization. The project charter will include the SLA and the targets established to deliver its border control procedures. The project charter is signed by the head of department or chief executive officer and authorizes the project manager to use organizational resources for the project. Once the design of the NSW is approved, each stakeholder must submit its own project charter. The NSW master plan and schedule are prepared based on commitments defined in the project charter.

Customs support. The customs agency is clearly the most important stakeholder since it is involved in practically all processes. The maximum possible support must be secured from customs. The time taken to do so will depend on the leadership and middle management. Experience has shown that the process can be extremely arduous, but when the NSW's role and how it can benefit customs operations are explained, support usually comes through eventually. Regular updates and meetings with customs senior management help dissipate concerns and misconceptions.

Nurturing the buy-in of senior policy makers. They have time constraints and interactions with them may be limited. Whatever time can be spent with them presents a precious opportunity to maintain a clear understanding of the NSW, share experiences, and bring up areas where their support is needed.

National single window versus cross-border regulatory agency. CBRAs are, understandably, extremely protective of their responsibilities. The clear and continuous message is that the CBRA role remains unchanged and that the NSW's mandate is to expedite CBRA processes. So many people are involved in the project and any misconceptions must be clarified.

Pilot tests. The project plan needs pilot tests before the system goes live. A few users (customs brokers, ship agents) run transactions through the system to validate processing as per specifications. After the pilot test, the project team meets with users to get their feedback.

Phased rollout. The NSW is usually implemented in three or more phases. Simpler features should be included in phase 1 and then be built up. Each phase should preferably not exceed 1 year. The shorter time frame of deliverables helps maintain support and commitment and secures confidence from all stakeholders in the project.

Scope creep. Once stakeholders understand the NSW's potential, they often request more functionality. Such scope creep can originate from team members, policy makers, and others. The PMU must control such requests and maintain a list of future enhancements. Proposals to increase features can come anytime during the project cycle. The request is accepted or rejected depending on whether it contributes to the key performance indicator (KPI). The proposed features often do not meet the criteria since KPI-related features are included in the project. Valid proposals for new features are assessed through a structured change control process as part of the project management methodology.

Procurement of national single window as a turnkey system. The procurement of the NSW system can proceed as a single bid for software and hardware; or two separate bids, one for software and then one for hardware. While both options are feasible, managing deliverables is simpler when the NSW is procured as a turnkey system consisting of software and hardware. Separate procurement—two separate suppliers, one for software and another for hardware—will often be challenging as problems that arise can be shifted by the software supplier to the hardware supplier or vice versa. The client then needs to arbitrate. With the turnkey approach, responsibility for problem resolution is clear and lies with the sole supplier.

Another approach is for a government ICT organization, together with subcontractors with specialized skills, to design and customize the NSW software. While technically feasible, the approach has substantial risks given the complexity of the NSW software. The organization must have software development experience, otherwise the project could have cost overruns and be delayed. The approach offers flexibility and potential cost savings for future enhancements.

Irrespective of the approach adopted to develop the NSW software, the NSW operator should consider setting up an in-house software development team to provide future enhancements. Skills transfer to the NSW operator in-house team should be a deliverable of the NSW software supplier.

Private sector involvement. The private sector must be continuously involved throughout the project life cycle to secure its buy-in and commitment. The private sector directly benefits from the NSW and is a rich source of practical knowledge on trade issues and requirements, adding significant value to the project. During the test phases, private sector entities usually volunteer to participate and run test cases to validate the new system.

Communications and branding. The introduction of the NSW significantly changes the trade and transport community. The PMU and the NSW operator must reach out regularly to the many stakeholders to clarify the NSW rationale, the impact on each stakeholder group, and the NSW benefits. A comprehensive communications program, using multiple channels, is required during project preparation, implementation, and operations. Branding is an effective means to focus on and clarify the NSW services. Effective project branding helps draw and maintain stakeholders' attention by capturing key ideas in simple precepts. Targeting specific stakeholder groups to ingrain the NSW rationale in their thinking, dispel any misconceptions, emphasize the benefits, and secure stakeholders' buy-in.

National Single Window Implementation by ADB Members

The table shows the status of World Trade Organization (WTO) members' national single window implementation. The information has been extracted from the WTO Trade Facilitation Agreement database (accessed October 2021). Some of the links may change and not be accessible.

1	Australia	Integrated Cargo System
2	Austria	It has no national legislation or measures in addition to the European Union (EU) notification: • EU single window initiative • European Commission • Directorate General for Taxation and Customs Union • The EU Single Window Environment for Customs
3	Cambodia	The national single window (NSW) has allowed traders to submit electronic licenses, permits, certificates, and others for import and export since July 2019. The NSW is connected to the United Nations' Automated System for Customs Data (ASYCUDA), which has operated since 2008. The initial implementation phase has been covered by five interministerial agencies: General Department of Customs and Excise, Ministry of Commerce, Council Development of Cambodia, Ministry of Health, and Ministry of Industry and Handicrafts. The NSW will improve the customs system and other regulatory government agencies. Through the Association of Southeast Asian Nations (ASEAN) Single Window, Cambodia has exchanged electronic documents with ASEAN member states, including the certificate of origin e-form D since July 2019 and ASEAN customs declaration documents since December 2020. Cambodia National Single Window
4	Canada	• Single Window Initiative • Other Government Departments Interface
5	People's Republic of China	China International Single Window
6	Denmark	It has no national legislation or measure in addition to the EU notification: • EU single window initiative • European Commission • Directorate General for Taxation and Customs Union • The EU Single Window Environment for Customs
7	Finland	• Port Traffic Declaration Service (Portnet) • Customs collection regulations

continued on next page

Table continued

8	France	Le guichet unique national du dédouanement (GUN)
9	Germany	It has no national legislation or measure in addition to the EU notification: • EU single window initiative • European Commission • Directorate General for Taxation and Customs Union • The EU Single Window Environment for Customs
10	Hong Kong, China	It launched phase 1 of the Trade Single Window in December 2018, which provides a voluntary e-option to lodge import and export documents through a single electronic platform. The single window covers 14 types of trade documents. Phase 2, extending the e-option to another 28 types of trade documents, is set to roll out by batches from 2023 onward. Hong Kong Trade Single Window
11	India	To ease doing business, the government's Single Window Interface for Facilitation of Trade (SWIFT) allows importers and exporters to lodge their clearance documents online at a single point. Required permission, if any, from other regulatory agencies is obtained online without the trader having to approach them separately. SWIFT has streamlined the entire process of consignment clearance and significantly reduced the interface between traders and regulatory agencies.[a] SWIFT SWIFT provides the following: • **Integrated declaration.** Traders submit integrated import and export declarations that contain clearance-related information required by all participating government agencies. Separate forms and declarations have been dispensed with. The integrated declaration is used by the major import regulatory agencies involved in issuing clearances or no-objection certificates for live consignments, i.e., post-import activities are under the ambit of a single import declaration and the online clearance facility. • **Integrated risk assessment.** All participating government agencies use an automated system to apply the principles of risk-based selectivity for inspection and testing. Customs already had a functional risk management system for risk-based selective interdiction of consignments. Now, risk criteria of major import and export regulatory agencies for interdiction, sampling, and testing of consignments are integrated into an integrated risk management system. • **Automated routing.** The system applies business rules to identify consignments based on the declaration to automatically route them to the relevant participating government agencies. • **Online clearance.** The system records and collates clearance-related decisions and approvals from all participating government agencies and delivers the results to the trader at a single point. An online system releases consignments to the major import and export regulatory participating government agencies. • **Paperless processing.** Traders can submit all consignment clearance supporting documents electronically with digital signatures. The trader need not approach the regulatory agencies with hard-copy documents, thereby making the entire process faceless and paperless.
12	Indonesia	Lembaga National Single Window provides the following services: • Document (customs declarations and licenses) validation and reconciliation • Indonesia National Trade Repository • Dwelling time dashboard • Document tracking (customs declarations, licenses, and electronic certificate of origin form D) • Call center and customer services
13	Ireland	It has no national legislation or measure in addition to EU notification: • EU single window initiative • European Commission • Directorate General for Taxation and Customs Union • The EU Single Window Environment for Customs

continued on next page

Table *continued*

14	Italy	Sportello Unico Doganale
15	Japan	Nippon Automated Cargo and Port Consolidated System
16	Kazakhstan	It has introduced a pilot version. The system will fully operate in several years.
17	Republic of Korea	Since March 2006, Uni-Pass has allowed electronic applications related to imports, exports, and other transactions without the user having to visit the agencies. As of May 2017, 26 agencies verifying 55 requirements had been linked to the single window system, which has processed 855,244 cases out of 896,960 (95.3%).
18	Kyrgyz Republic	The Tulpar System allows those involved in foreign trade to electronically submit information demanded by supervisory authorities for import, export, and transit operations.
19	Lao People's Democratic Republic	The single window is being piloted by the National Committee on Single Window Establishment, chaired by the vice-minister of finance, based on the Decision on the Implementation and Operation for the Development, Implementation and Operation of National Single Window on Customs Procedures No. 2109, Ministry of Finance, 26 June 2015.
20	Luxembourg	International Trade Single Window for Logistics
21	Malaysia	Malaysia NSW has been in operation since 2009 through the myTradeLink web portal.
22	New Zealand	Since 6 July 2015, approved customs brokers have been able to apply for supplier and client codes using the Trade Single Window (TSW) Online Registration. The e-commerce platform for trade—part of the Customs and Ministry for Primary Industries Joint Border Management System program—will allow all border requirements for goods to be met in one place. The improved TSW, in place since 2013 and with more than 5 million transactions processed, supports seamless clearance of trade. The TSW has expanded functionality across the system. TSW online registration allows brokers and other organizations to control who can do what in their name.
23	Norway	• Norwegian Customs (TVINN) for import and export declaration and collection of statistics • Safe Sea Net for maritime traffic • AltInn, the main portal for contact between citizens and government agencies, including border agencies
24	Portugal	Serviços Aduaneiros
25	Singapore	What You Need to Know about TradeNet is a platform for trade and logistics partners to transact digitally for domestic and cross-border regulatory trade processes. To enable digital data reuse across the various trade-related transactions on the Networked Trade Platform, TradeNet is integrated within and accessible via the platform.
26	Spain	Agencia Tributaria, Ventanilla Única Aduanera.

continued on next page

Table *continued*

27	Sweden	Tullverket
28	Switzerland	Only one government authority is at the border: customs. It is responsible for enforcing about 150 non-customs decrees. The duties include formal checks of goods, release of goods only after submission of a permit (issued by another authority), or refusal to import or export certain goods. The one-stop shop at all customs offices with a physical single window is supported by information and communication technology. A full-fledged electronic single window will be put in place in the coming years. See DaziT transformation programme.
29	Tajikistan	The pilot version of the single window system was launched on 8 November 2019. The implementation deadline is 22 December 2023.
30	Thailand	Thailand National Single Window
31	Turkey	Read about the single window and the port single window
32	United Kingdom	The government has initiated work on what a single trade window would look like and what benefits and outcomes for traders, industry, and government could be achieved. The program is being designed.
33	United States	The government implements the single window through the Automated Commercial Environment, the primary system for processing trade-related import and export data required by government agencies. The transition away from paper-based procedures has streamlined processes for government and industry.
34	Viet Nam	Trading companies submit their declarations for the export and import of goods to the national single window, which automatically produces the results needed by trading and customs to expedite the clearance of goods. The system has integrated 174 administrative procedures of 13 ministries and agencies, or 2.3 million entries from 30,900 enterprises. Viet Nam UNNExT will continue to develop the NSW IT system to connect all related government agencies and stakeholders in the supply chain, including banks, insurance companies, import and export companies, and logistics operators.

[a] WTO. *Trade Facilitation Agreement Database: Operation of the Single Window.* https://tfadatabase.org/members/india/article-10-4-3.

References

The United Nations Economic Commission for Europe (UNECE) is the international focal point for trade facilitation recommendations and standards and develops instruments to reduce, harmonize, and automate procedures and paperwork in international trade. The UNECE's work is supported by the UN Centre for Trade Facilitation and Electronic Business (UN/CEFACT), which has developed and maintained a suite of products to help establish a single window. The following deal with the main technical aspects of the single window:

- UN/CEFACT. 2005. *Recommendation No. 33. Recommendation and Guidelines on Establishing a Single Window.* Geneva.
- UN/CEFACT. 2009. *Single Window Repository.* Part I. Geneva.
- UN/CEFACT. 2010. *Recommendation No. 35. Establishing a Legal Framework for the International Trade Single Window.* Geneva.
- UN/CEFACT. 2013. *Recommendation No. 34. Data Simplification and Standardization for International Trade.* Geneva.
- UN/CEFACT. 2017. *Terminology for Single Window and Other ePlatforms.* Version 1. Geneva.
- UN/CEFACT. 2020. *Recommendation No. 33. Recommendation and Guidelines on Establishing a Single Window.* Geneva.

The UN Economic and Social Commission for Asia and the Pacific (UNESCAP) is the regional focal point and coordinator for trade facilitation capacity building and technical assistance in Asia and the Pacific. UNESCAP has a long-standing program on trade facilitation and is the secretariat for the United Nations Network of Experts for Paperless Trade and Transport in Asia and the Pacific (UNNExT). UNESCAP and UNNExT have prepared the following technical and practical guides on national single window (NSW) design and implementation:

- UNESCAP. 2009. *Business Process Analysis Guide to Simplify Trade Procedures.* Bangkok.
- UNNExT. 2010. Towards a Single Window Trading Environment Best Practice in Single Window Implementation: Case of Singapore's TradeNet. *Brief No. 2.* March.
- UNNExT. 2011. Towards a Single Window Trading Environment—Achieving Effective Stakeholder Involvement. *Brief No. 7.* September. UNESCAP. 2012. *Data Harmonization and Modeling Guide for Single Window Environment.* Bangkok.
- UNESCAP. 2012. *Electronic Single Window Legal Issues – A Capacity Building Guide.* Bangkok.
- UNESCAP. 2012. *Single Window Planning and Implementation Guide.* Bangkok.
- UNESCAP. 2018. *Single Window for Trade Facilitation: Regional Best Practices and Future Development.* Bangkok.
- UNESCAP. 2021. *Cross-Border E-Trade: The ASEAN Single Window.* Bangkok.
- UNNExT. Towards a Single Window Trading Environment. *Brief No. 1.* November.

The World Customs Organization (WCO) promotes the implementation of the NSW and has prepared the following guides on NSW design and implementation, focusing on customs administration:

- WCO. 2007. *WCO Data Model, Single Window Data Harmonization.* Brussels.
- WCO. 2011. A Survey of Single Window Implementation. *WCO Research Paper.* 17. Brussels.
- WCO. 2017. *Building a Single Window Environment.* Volume 1. Brussels.
- WCO. 2017. *Building a Single Window Environment.* Volume 2. Brussels.
- WCO. 2017. *Building a Single Window Environment—Integrated Risk Management.* Part VIII, volume 2. Brussels.
- WCO. 2018. *Coordinated Border Management.* Brussels.

Other References

Asian Development Bank. 2019. *Potential Exports and Nontariff Barriers to Trade—Maldives National Study.* Manila.

Asia-Pacific Economic Cooperation Policy Support Unit. 2018. *Study on Single Window Systems International Interoperability.* Singapore.

European Union. 2017. *New European Interoperability Framework.* Brussels.

Harvard Business School. 1995. *Singapore TradeNet: A Tale of One City*. Cambridge, MA.

Inter-American Development Bank. What is RedVUCE?

Organisation for Economic Co-operation and Development. 2018. *Trade Facilitation and the Global Economy.* Paris.

Teo, H., B. Tan, and K. Wei. 1997. Organizational Transformation Using Electronic Data Interchange: The Case of TradeNet in Singapore. *Journal of Management Information Systems.* 13 (4).

UN/CEFACT. 2018. *Reference Data Model, White Paper.* Geneva.

UN Economic Commission for Africa 2011. Technology in Government in Africa: TIGA Awards.

UNNExT. 2011. *Japan's Development of a Single Window—Case of Nippon Airport Cargo Community System.* Bangkok.

World Bank. 2005. Implementation Completion Report (SCL-44750 TF-25327) Tunisia Export Development Project, Report 31785. Washington, DC.

World Bank. 2012. Collaborative Border Management: A New Approach to an Old Problem. *Economic Premise.* 78.

World Trade Organization. 2014. *Trade Facilitation Agreement.*

Lightning Source UK Ltd.
Milton Keynes UK
UKHW051952300522
403760UK00015B/285